MOTHER, MAY I?

Alma Villanueva

MOTHER, MAY I?

Copyright 1978 by Alma Villanueva.
All rights reserved.

| We have moved & our new address is: | RELAMPAGO BOOKS
601 ARBOR CIRCLE
AUSTIN, TEXAS 78745
PHONE (512) 447-4049 |

First printing, October, 1978
by Motheroot Publications

cover sculpture: Judith Joinville
cover photo: Wilfredo Q. Castano
back cover photo: Antoinette Goulet
editor: Mary Allison Rylands

*To my mother, my daughter
and Judith*

Part I   1.

I was always fascinated
with lights then,
with my hands
with my fingers
with my fingertips, because

if I squinted my eyes at them
lights sprayed off
burst off
and a joy burst inside me
and it felt good on my
eyes to see it, so

I squinted my eyes at
everything in this manner
and everything had joy
on it, in it. it was
my secret. only

my grandma knew. I knew
she knew by the way
she looked at things
long and slow and peaceful
and her face would shine, lights
all over, coming out of
her tiniest wrinkles;
she became a young girl.
there were things that could not
shine lights. we
avoided these. these things
had no joy
gave no joy. these things
took joy. these things
could make you old. I didn't
know it then, but

these things were death.

The Dead

The cement seems to go forever
but it ends at the ocean. I've
seen it
and this is true. we sit
in big buildings, with
hard benches
and everyone is scared
and the lady talks
and her eyes don't see you. we
don't look at her too long. I
watch her mouth move,
move. she has a tongue. but

I know she's dead. I
can't feel her.

- - - - - - - - - - - - - - - - - -

I like to play outside
with my panties off; the
air feels so good between
my legs. I
love to swing and spread them
wide. I
love to put my dolly's hand
there
and make her tickle me. we
make tents and hide
and sometimes the Tickle Man
gets me. but I
like him to. I
let him. when I
have to go to school I
go to the bathroom
and he finds me. he is
like my uncle but
he stops when

6

I say stop.
bathrooms are nice. no
one wants to look at
you then. later
they ask—what took
   you so long?—but
that's when you make things, I
think, like having babies; I
hear them talking sometimes:
   —you have to push it out
hard.—I do that. I
like to look at what I
make. it even smells
good to me. sometimes
they're pretty, when you eat
too fast
and the corn comes right out.
it makes it yellow. one
time my aunt came in and I
peed and pooped and I
said—I just made a
   salad.—she didn't
look too happy. so I kept
it to myself. and I used
to swallow my tiny rubber
dolly and have a baby in my
poop. I loved to find it. my
grandma found me doing it. she
wasn't mad. she smiled
a little. she said
   —it'll get stuck and grow as big
as you and you won't have any room
   left.—so
I stopped.
and she made me wear long pants
under my dresses so she
would know the wind
couldn't smell me.

and then I learned how
to hide.

2.

my mother was beautiful.
she smelled good.
she put perfume on her panties
and her legs were smooth. they
sounded funny but they
felt slippery.
she had lots of boyfriends.
lots.
my mother was beautiful.
sometimes I slept in the kitchen
on chairs so
he could sleep with her.
sometimes I kissed her just like
he did.
she was always going away
with one of *them*.
she was always beautiful
for *them*.
and sometimes I cried for my
father but I didn't know who
he was.

playing

I am little and I sleep with you.
we pretend.
we pretend, I'm the mother
and you're the little girl
and you cry for me cause I
have to go to work and you
have to stay. I

laugh at you, big cry baby. I
go away and you pull me back

by my leg and we
laugh and laugh
till it's time to
get up.

3.

my grandmother takes me to the first
day of school. everyone speaks
so fast. I can read and count
in spanish. I can say two poems
in spanish. you can't speak
spanish here. they don't like
it and the teacher is fat
and so white
and I don't like her. I run
home and my grandma says I can
stay. we
go to movies and chinatown and shopping.
she holds one side of the shopping bag, I
hold the other. we
pray and dunk *pan dulce* in coffee. we
make tortillas together. we
laugh and take the buses
everywhere. when we
go to the movies she cries and
she dances when she irons. I
comb her long hair and rub her
back with alcohol. one time
before we left the house, we
said our prayer and she was looking
for her hat and she was wearing
it and I
started to laugh and laugh and I
couldn't stop and she found
it on her head
and she spat—*grosera!*—and it
made me laugh harder and she gave
me the hand that meant a spanking

(and she never spanked me)
and she laughed too.
and when I flew she always
woke me gently—so the soul
   and the body will stay.—and I
loved to fly
and dream. I was
always the strongest and the fastest. we
always said our dreams. she said
she knew when her four babies
were dying because they always
pointed up with their fingers
and they'd die in the night.
and I think she dressed me too warmly
and woke me gently
to trick death
to let me stay.

Dreaming

the danger of flying
is coming back. you must
close your eyes. one
time I didn't and I saw me
laying there and I didn't like me
and I didn't want to come
back. I thought she
was disgusting. she
had to eat and everything. she
was stuck. I
wasn't. I came
back anyway and then she
stood up and looked in the mirror
and scared me
to life.
- - - - - - - - - - - - -
but I kept dreaming, no matter
how stubborn
she was.

4.

I watch you put lipstick
on, red and beautiful, you
press your lips together
to make it stick
and I
grab you
and kiss you
on the lips with my
mouth open—is this
　how they do it,
mother?—
I ask
I wish
to be closer
to you
than lips or lipstick
or skin
I wish
to kiss

your womb.

playing

the pretend
place
is bed, we
lay together, you
tell me stories
about when you were
little and you were
bad, I
laugh and laugh
and we
are both 5
and no one's
the mother. we

hide from the
grown ups,

playing.
- - - - - - - -
I think one time we
never switched
back and I stayed
your
mother and I stayed
bigger and I stayed
stronger, to take
care of you,
mother, we

forgot the world is bigger than
our bed.

5.

the nun asked to look at
my hands. I thought she thought
they were beautiful, so I
put them out
and she hit them with
a ruler. it hurt it hurt
and she told me to
put them out
again and I wouldn't and she
tried to grab my hands so
I grabbed the ruler and hit
her and ran
home and my grandma let me
stay when she saw
my hands. there was
a beautiful young nun who
spoke spanish and english and she
sat in the dark on the other
side of the cage. the metal was black

and cold and beautiful. it had flowers
and I loved to put my face on it, it
felt so good and cold.
and when she came and sat and spoke
her voice was very warm. she
said she came from mexico. I
bet she didn't let them shave
her head. this boy who was
very bad sat behind me
and he put his fingers in my *nalgas*
when we prayed and when I turned
and stared at him, he'd
smell them and smile. he
whispered one time in the yard
   —they all have bald heads.—

6.

I had a best friend who I loved
a lot. she was older
than me. she was bigger
but I was smarter
because I always
beat her in checkers. we were
playing in the park. we were
all alone and a man
came and said it was against
the law. we were
afraid and he said one of
us would have to go with him to
sign a book and Peggy said
   —she'll go.—and I thought, well
that's because I'm smarter than
her, so I went and Peggy ran
home. all of a sudden he picked
me up and he wouldn't put
me down and I told him
   —see this dress? my mother
bought it for me. she

has lots of money. she'll
  give you money
  if you let me
go. look! my dress is pretty
and new!—I'd been showing
off that day twirling in circles
pretending
I was kidnapped from a king
and queen
pretending
I was rich
because my dress was so beautiful.

he put me down.
he took off my dress.
he took off my t-shirt.
he took off my panties.
and then he said
  —do you want to suck something
    good?—
and I thought it must be bad.
it must be licorice because
I hate it because
he hates me and
he wants me to eat
something bad and maybe
if I eat something bad
he'll let me go. so I said
  —o.k.—
he put it in my mouth
and it didn't taste like anything.
it hurt my mouth but I
wouldn't cry and then
he made me lie down
and the stickers hurt
and I was getting all dirty
and I knew if I cried
he'd kill me. then
he put his fingers
there

and it hurt
and I almost screamed
but I didn't because I knew
he'd kill me. and
he touched me all over
 and I lay there
and I didn't cry.
and I knew he could kill me if
he wanted to.
and I didn't care anymore.
he said
    —if I let you go, do you
      promise not to tell
      anyone? because
      if you do
I'll kill you.—
I didn't care.
I just said
    —I promise.—
and when he let me go I didn't run.
I walked.
and when my aunt saw me she said
Peggy told her and the police were
finding me and I told her
    —I always have to do the dirty
work.—
and I didn't cry.

it was then I decided to become a boy.

7.

I've found the rooftops.
I've found the fences.
I've found the highest rock
and I've sat on it.
I've found the secret places
in Golden Gate Park
and listened to voices.

15

I've found the ocean
and reached it, riding
my own bike.
I've found unmade buildings
and sat on the highest steel.
I bled there the first time
and knew it was special, but
I ignored it.
I fought the toughest boy
in school and
I made his nose bleed.
I play football and they pick me
first or second.
I climbed the statue on Dolores
street and sat on the horse
and couldn't get down
for hours. 2 people ask me
if I need help and
I say NO so
I jump and my feet burn but
I don't cry.
I saw my stepfather strangling
my mother, so
I broke the window
and hit him with an ashtray.
he fell.
I hated him. my mother had my brother.
I loved him.
I change his diapers.
I sing him to sleep.
I take him down to the park
and don't let anyone
touch him. we live
in projects. we live
in hotels. then she
gives me away

to strangers.

8.

my grandma is too old
they say.
they say she can't
cook anymore or
sweep anymore or
iron anymore or
dance anymore. I know
they're wrong. can
she help it if
she sees death waiting
in the same car every night?
she looks out the window
and he looks up at her
and stares.
she isn't scared. she just knows
she's old.
she forgets and tells them
these things and
they put her in Laguna Honda.
they give her away
to strangers

too.

9.

I visit her there and I hate it.
I walk down the hall where the
elevator lets you out
and old people sit on the
hard benches, on both
sides, staring,
staring. and they smell
like death cause they're
scared and
I hate it. grandma doesn't
smell, she's mad all

the time. she complains
too much, they say.
I bring her chilis and onions
and comb her hair
and rub her back
and she laughs, but her eyes
her eyes

10.

grandma said—when a dog howls
  in the daytime someone
  is dying.—they called
my aunt and said she
was dying, so we went
my aunt, my mother
and I. we went
but they said she

was dead already but
I didn't believe them so
I ran in and they were lying
again because
she sat up
and said
  —Alma, *no me quiero morir*—*
and then she died.
                      AIIIIIIIII MAMACITA
mamacita
and then I cried.
and they all ran in
my aunt, my mother, the doctor
and they didn't believe me
and I couldn't stop crying so
they made me stop with some medicine
and I didn't cry again.
I didn't cry that night.
or the next day.
or the funeral day.

what I did
was drop one rose
into the hole
and I felt it squish
and they thought I was selfish
and stubborn because
I dressed up in my new shoes
and a skirt and a red shirt
and I didn't cry.

they didn't know the rose
was me.

                *Alma, I don't want to die.

Part 2   11.

this family checks for lice.
this family says
        I don't appreciate a
        decent home.
this family makes me sleep separate
from
    their children.
this family says I steal.
        I don't.
this family has no mother or
father just
like me. a lady
gives out 1 frozen Twinkie
each
for lunches. we are
all orphans. I run

away to my aunt's
and she keeps me for

awhile. I get
mumps and I lay there
and cross my arms
and see lights spraying
off
my hands.
my feet. I eat

tortillas again. I am
happy. my aunt
and I talk and talk, in
spanish, in
english, we laugh, but
she doesn't dance. there

is a greyness on my eyes. it
goes away when I'm alone. my
aunt lives in the projects by
the bay. there is
a place by
the water where
rocks are. there are
voices there. I see
lights on
the water and
the rocks
and the lights
make the greyness go
away. there is
a place
inside
me they
cannot enter. that is
where

I'm hiding.

12. (about 13)

I sleep all day.
I sleep all night.
I do not eat. much.
I do not talk. much.

my eyes are yellow.
my gums bleed.
I cannot roam
and play. they
found out.
I'm a girl. they
expose themselves. they
follow me. they
do not leave me
alone. they
stare
with their dead
eyes. they
speak
with their dead
mouths. there

is one who
is different. a
boy. —you
  will die
  if you
  don't start
eating— the
doctor says.
I eat.
we walk, the
boy and I.
we speak, the
boy and I.
we laugh, the
boy and I.
we kiss, the
boy and I.
approaching,

gently, dreaming, softly, child to child,
we love
on rooftops, doorways, parks, alleys
we love, the
boy and I. and

a child blooms
inside me.

13.

I am alone again.
—I can't marry you. they
　won't let me. they
　say,
she'll have 12 more
kids in 10 years, you
know those people.
　　　　　　　　they
　say
　NO.—
we walk.
we cry. (the
boy cries)
I am alone again, but

a fullness starts.

14.

I speak to you.
we sleep together.
your tiny foot
moves, one side to
the other. my mother
keeps me,
　—we women stick together.— she
tells
the clinic secretary

    —*she* didn't want to marry *him*.—
I prepare for you.
I buy tiny shirts (are
you really there?)
I buy a crib (are
you really there?)
I buy pink, pink, pink (a
daughter, a daughter?)
we lay together
at night (could I
keep you
inside
me forever?), little
comfort. tiny foot.

15.

it starts. the
pain. my
mother and a friend, we
drink screwdrivers and we
walk to the hospital (2
blocks) a little drunk
and laughing. my friend and
I can't believe I'm
staying. my
mother does. the
nuns don't approve
of screwdrivers or
laughing. they
put me in a room
to wait for
pain. I

get up and walk. they
tell me to lie
down. they
leave and I
get up and walk and look

out the window. they
are angry
and give me a shot. I

wake up to
pain like
death. it is
morning and white and cold
and their knives and needles
hurt me. I

give birth dreaming.

16.

another child. we
marry. we
sneak. (we
are still
too young) me
in black. he
in uniform. he
stays 2 nights
and then goes
for 2 years to
their armies, their guns, their prisons, their death—

again,
they pull my child from
me. numbed from
the waist down
the doctor watching
the clock (he is late for
something)
the water bursts
the head shoving (but they
pull him out
anyway)
the time

the time
but I trick them.
I give birth dreaming,

again.

17.

he comes back, the
boy/man.
he does not cry
so easily.
he does not laugh
so easily.
he drinks too much
and
he hurts me sometimes.
he is angry about
something.
he wants to kill
something. but when
we make love
we are children
again.
he is my sun, I
turn and turn toward
him. I
give birth

to a son.

birthing

this is the way to trick
the dead. by
birthing, by
birthing.
this is the way to trick
the living. by

dreaming, by
dreaming.
watch out, Alma.
watch out, Alma. you
don't trick
yourself.

18.

and then began the years
of silence, the years
my mouth would open
and no words would
speak,
my mouth locked tight.
and a loneliness grew

that I couldn't name.

19.

I looked for it
in my husband's eyes.
I looked for it
in my children's eyes.
I looked for it
in supermarkets.
I looked for it
in the oven.
I looked for it
in the dustpan.
I looked for it
in the sink.
in the tv.
in the washing machine.
in the car.
in the streets.
in the cracks
of my linoleum. I polished

and cleaned and cared for everything
silently. I put on my masks, my
costumes and posed for each
occasion. I conducted myself
well, I think, but
an emptiness
grew
that no thing
could fill. I think

I hungered for myself.

20.

the last diapers are thrown
away. (the baby is grown)
the husband is locked
away. (the husband is crazy)
will someone change
my diapers?
will someone lock
me in?
he sees things in the dark
at night. I turn
on the light and make it go
away. my children have
nightmares and cry for me. I tell them
I'm here. I lay
in the bed coiled up like a fetus, no thing
out
there can comfort me. I uncoil
and stand
and feed the children. no one
knows

I'm a liar.

21.

we look for you, my

husband and I
we look for you till
I'm dizzy. are you
here, mamacita? are you
here? he says—here
it is.—he's found
you, a '13'
in the ground. they said
—Jesus Villanueva
is '13'.—
I touch the
one, the
three.
I begin to cry
and no one stops
me. I didn't
know it but
a seed spilled out
and my mouth
ate it. I think

that's when the rose took root.

22.

when she left this man she thought
she'd die.
but she didn't. she thought
the sun would go out
but it didn't.
and she heard a voice, distant
and small, but
she heard it.
and her mouth opened slightly
and a word spilled out. the word

was 'I'.

inside

I am here. (do
you hear me?) hear
me. hear me.
I am here. birthing
(yourself) is
no easy task.
I am here. (pleading)
I am here. (teasing)
I am here. (taunting)
I am here. (simply)
I am here.

Part 3   23.

it began
with the death of
her friend
and she took
her friend's husband
and she took
her friend's children
and her own
and they all
moved

to the country
to the trees
to the grass
to the hay
to the honeysuckle
to the daffodils
   in spring
to the naked ladies
   in fall
to the full creek

  in winter
to the tall corn
  in summer
to the fresh lettuce
to the red tomato, apple
to the plump chickens
to their fresh eggs
to the turkey vulture
to the red-tailed hawk
to the great blue heron
  under the bridge
to the steer in the field (we
  ate him)
to the pigs in the pen (we
  ate them
too)
to the frogs in the creek
  that drown out
the night
to the wild turkey
  my son never
caught
to the plump quail
  we've never
tasted
to the frost on the bridge
  on the leaves
  on the trough
  on the spider's web
    with its millions
of stars
to the blossoming trees
  that scatter
like snow
to the dying leaves
  that warm
the ground
to the pruning of trees
to the plowing of earth

to the turn
to the turn

of the seasons.

24.

and she went in, carefully.
she went in, cautiously.
she went in, trembling.
she went in,

alone.

Her myth (of creation)

it was dark, so dark
I was lost, so I
lay down flat
in my fear

and dark figures
with bleeding bodies
and staring eyes
with voiceless mouths

came to me
and I lay flat
with fear
till I realized they

were me. the dead.
and when I realized this,
a light burst through
the roof (I thought

I was on the highest
mountain on earth
looking, looking
with a shift

of my eyes) and the light
blinded me, so
I closed them. then I really
saw and

I was no longer afraid.
I did not weep.
I did not laugh.
I was not old.
I was not young.
"I am here."

I said.

25.

it began
with the death of
a friend
and it ended
with the death of
another. this made
her angry
and she told the
man "I'm not going to die!"
and she told the
doctor (who wanted her
womb) "I'm not going to die!"
and I think they believed
her. she
was angry. so
the man, the doctor
and death
got scared

and left.

life cycle (up to 32)

some men carry birth

(my first husband went
   crazy with
it)
some men carry death
(my second sucks on it
   like a bone, like
a bone)
I carry both. I'm
a juggler.

I'm a juggler.

26.

meanwhile,
the daughter had grown
and she loved her. (a
woman, a woman) they
endured the rebellions, the
jealousies of a mother, a
daughter, as
she had with
her mother. they mouthed
the same curses
she and her mother
mouthed "bitch, whore" the
unnameables, the
unutterables you say
to those you love, to
your mother, that bitch, to
your daughter, that whore
   of a girl

I love you.

the proof (about 33)

I've shrunk down
and kissed

my womb
and heard
my heart
and listened
to mothers
and daughters
everywhere.

I've grown back,
little mother,
with my child's heart
beating
with my woman's womb
birthing
mothers, daughters
everywhere. we
sit and stare. your
eye, a camera, my
eye, a camera,
the photograph
is love.

                    to mom

27.

it is not easy to
end here.
it would be
a lie.
the sons are growing
too.
one is bigger and stronger
than me
and he loves me. (we
aren't passionate and furious, like
a mother, a daughter)
there are 3 little sons, my friend's
and my own. they look

at me with
tender eyes (sometimes). they are
boys who will be
men. and

I love them.

the thread (the amputation)

the thread is bloodstained. I
gave it to you, as my
mother to me, as her
mother to her
and it is thick with
blood, with life
and we are thick with
each other, my
daughter. my

daughter, my
girl; you
stand, staring
with your knife's
amputation: your
hands bloody: it
is your amputation—I
took it from my
mother: you
take it from
me—blood, my
daughter. love, my
daughter. life, my
daughter: life. now,

go and play.
become your
own mother
and spin your own lovely
thread.
        To Toni

28.

she awoke
and liked it.
she breathes breath
with a capital B.
she eats food
with a capital F.
she feels life
with a capital L.
she wants a man
with a capital M.
she wants love
with a capital L.O.V.E.
she wants to play
with a capital P.
is that asking

Too Much?

29.

he approaches, juggling
his words "would
           you
           like to
           dance?"
"sure." I
say.

mother, may I?

don't mistake my reassuring
words
for wisdom;
don't mistake my soothing
eyes
for peace;

we are
in such a large large
world
I've
learned the ropes
I've
cultivated my gardens
I've combed my shores
I've
played house
played god
created universes
in my kitchen
in my womb
and when I
hide I
play mother
to my own
little girl. I

was always
good at
make believe. all
I ask is
  may
I play?

epilogue

as in all
stories, there is a
story within a
story. there is the
story of my friend (the
one who walked
with me to the
hospital; she was why
I beat up the
toughest boy in school,

because he was going
to beat her up; she was my
best friend since 12; she still
is) who somehow
is always
there. her soft
eyes always
recognize
me.
(mom)

men come
and go. your friends

stay. women
stay. mom
said. perhaps

this is a story of
women raging against
women; of
women loving
women; of
women listening to
women, because
men don't have time
to because
men move
on, because
men haven't learned
how to
listen, to
speak as
women; so

the thread, the story
connects
between women;
grandmothers, mothers, daughters,

the women
the thread of this
story.

(mamacita)

when a man opens a woman, she
is like a rose, she
will never close
again.

ever.

(me)

pistils. stamens.
wavering in the sun.
a bloom on the bush.
a mixed bloom.
they wonder at it.
a bastard rose.
a wild rose.
colors gone mad.
a rupture of thorns.
you must not pluck it.
you must recognize
  a magic rose
         when
you see it.

        (excerpted from my poem
        Legacies and Bastard Roses)